M

Hannah Brooks-Motl

The Song Cave

Published by The Song Cave
www.the-song-cave.com

Design and layout by Mary Austin Speaker
Cover drawing by Stacy Jo Scott

ISBN:978-0-9967786-0-2
Library of Congress Control Number: 2015952752

FIRST EDITION

CONTENTS

for Dan

As the centuries go by, there is always a crowd before that picture, gazing into its depths, seeing their own faces reflected in it, seeing more the longer they look, never being able to say quite what it is that they see.

VIRGINIA WOOLF, "MONTAIGNE"

I went into M and read there

"If I'd written
to seek the world's favor"

and if I'd written—

To be strong I thought a lot of different things

POEM FOR M

I came upon a horse in a field; the barn was abandoned behind. Who was I to question the performance?

Living alone out here, I was small in the eye.

Wore a giant trouser and swung around: there was nothing down in the cave.

Yet would I be a better writer if I walked more in the woods?

The good smell off the night.

The rage—the flash—the gesturing

Things happen, M counseled, and tragedy you see vs tragedy you don't.

So when M begins drinking at five it is with a great deal of self-possession.

But when M gets wasted on one glass of red wine this also is civilized.

Sometimes M wonders why am I so faraway? And I go, you are close in spirit.

Persist in the little way of adjacency.

Of the burning light of the past, its unknown flickering—I transmit no mention and no lie.

Yet all thought is autobiographical, isn't it?

Persists in the little way of mind.

FEELINGS OF OF

OF SADNESS

An accidental failing, or unseasonable surprise—

"A stupid and monstrous ornament!"

There's no unfreezing the shock, it's not a moment or cart

I'm not brimmed with it yet

Ceasing the habit of speech almost completely

Or vivid with misdirection, and love

"The hot alarm of some very bad news"

I might cover my face

Circle the rocks

OF IDLENESS

So in rooms all day and night long
on tablets figuring memory, applying the family, at my job
over coffee, listening to sex—

    definition expands
    under languor
    becomes possible

★

With an audible subject I am which and the making of these
    "Mere shapeless masses and lumps of flesh"

                No fixed goal but the hither and yon, vague field
    of firework boom

        In glass books of time
    "I put them in writing"

★

In some passion "hoping to make my mind
    ashamed of itself"—

    so boredom
    wrapping his cock
    forced my jaw

OF PROMPT OR SLOW SPEECH

Facility and promptness, I have felt them
Burn many times, my face burned
And my belly—a kind of obliging I set flaming in halls
Was I speaking?
I was stoking my eye's fire
With familiar surprise, some dialogic vigor
Myself at a desk in an office
Inviting discourse
But all these things I did not slew
Because I proceed with deliberation, a kind of dumbness
Or mouth stuffed from want
Because I clack I whine
"Overcome by a listener"

OF PROGNOSTICATIONS

On the driveway caressing an innermost self
I picked up a sharpie and drew on my hand—an honest happening
It meant nothing

Once I had fallen in love, once out of
My dumb hand, fat star
And systems of terrible odds

"By spirits, bodily traits, dreams, and the like"
My ancestors work a public gloss
Their great fond wagers

All infinite, all common:
"A husband-man, digging very deep"
Hits the white

OF CONSTANCY

"Emerging from the shelter of a windmill": a glimpse of marquis de Gaust, spotted by seigneur de Bonneval, atop an amphitheater in Arles, he is walking the ruin. And aimed a culverin at, and lit the match of one to. In purple-colored fear the marquis blooms and moves, "turning pale and tightening up." Even the moderate Stoic consents to tremble: "Wear trouble, no remedy."

Standing in the downpour the marquis inclined a turn of phrase, a useless flowing.

Lavender waves away the world today, every power.

OF THE PUNISHMENT OF COWARDICE

Taking shame well onto myself, how like Naugahyde this felt

Draping funnily enough my shame and some report, of a lord:
"We might produce the same nature"

So I babied, then fled

Waving flowers, spilled in a woman's attire
"Declared ignoble, taxable, for ever useless at arms"

And marching past with equal fervor, an opposite fervor—
I took down my hand

OF FEAR

"Because terror enforces oblivion"

"It is an archipelago beneath scrutiny"

★

"Who to watch with a beady eye and report to the police"

"These mystical abominations to make me and mine fear"

"Until we lose this overwhelming sense of fear"

"Those in pressing fear of it, losing capacity"

"I offered what was clearly the wrong advice"

"I voted 'fear both equally' "

★

"Its very mistakes justify further expansion of the apparatus"

"Or have we run up against the limits of the possible"

★

"Now fear gives wings to our heels as in the above examples"

"Now it nails down and fetters our feet"

"Moreover, it exceeds all other disorders in intensity"

★

"As for the question how does one argue, I think one argues in
the usual way"

"At all events it is a strange passion"

"They call these panic terrors"

OF THE POWER OF THE IMAGINATION

"My art is to escape, not resist it"
lead you away
through the fog

Going in a gapped way and lucky into each room, take out your
knack
flat, elaborate, gold
harnessed so that body might leap
through its soul, leap
from the notion I became you

Down the mind-ridden road you held strangely
a small flock, and confabulation
rubbing the skies
our heads travel softly
birthing monsters and turning
kings turned to queens
godless to god

The horns
I used against you

From my walk
I imagined myself to a climax, extending around and leaf

was in climax, my fingers
all eyes

Invention got big
in the world
and bigger

I am making behavior
and motives
"as well in shadow as in substance"
the light streaming
in outline so rare and memorable
I made it

Wild with making

Trickery
swallow the real

OF CUSTOM, AND NOT EASILY CHANGING AN ACCEPTED LAW

In fear of innovation one grew

Something from another vat

"Nothing that custom will or cannot do"

Like the law to go into, almost vacant, a church

Where ugliness depends on itself

Where men piss squatting, do women walk backward to dawn

Or live on spiders and make provision of them

Where fire is the annual present

"Is it they who make the echo we hear"

Beat, then disturb

This motor

OF PEDANTRY

Across many years I bore a firm savor, scattered my pinkish
    beak, how showy
And a little nut, my gathering
"Like chits that have no other use than to be counted and
    thrown away"
Some gusty talk
Also filling
To learn what would not go in
How letter-struck they looked at me—it was teaching
To ride there, a marvel
"Knowledge is a good drug" and dialectic—and war-like
    enough, never begging
"A parrot could well say as much"
Like the arm of another, the book

My book in a horde

OF FRIENDSHIP

"My ability doesn't go far enough to undertake a rich, polished
picture"

So I doodled around her, "a lovely woman

Tapering off to a fish"

She flapped to the corner and wrote there

Have you noticed her empty

How a better hand waves

Then I try

*

From the apartment we flattened paths to the trees

Sunlight on the quiet between us

I gathered up our inclinations

Returned to my description

How seldom we all are I felt wearing her coat—

"Because it was she, because it was I"

And then by the years I held her in fabulous net

Wearing her jacket we shook from the winter

"Embraced each other by our names"

And danced in the regular rooms

In loving, in play

I have shirked

★

“Walk in those other friendships bridle in hand, not so well tied”

Go where the action is clean, in passion

To learn “the secret to reveal to no other man”

Even doubled my soul

“Nothing bitter or stinging about it”

We plunged the mixture of us

Walking free

*

And at the edge of the plot

It required many names

It sat up on the couch

It entered the singing

With shy mouth it belonged there

29 SONNETS

OF ETIENNE DE LA BOETIE

Madame I blasted

"Madame, I offer nothing of my own"

In far richer hand

From the sky

What is black

But pond, village, the hills

Blunt pulses of love

Or more dedications

Madame I drafted

To the heart

It was twitchy

"In his greenest youth"

And bled there

JOY, SIGN, AUTUMN STAR

"THERE IS NO MAN WHO HAS LESS BUSINESS TALKING OF MEMORY"

In a town made of trash I meet a small woods, folded or draped.
    And this "all furnished with matter."

An island I make because I must cede to image. The town's a
    disguise or the drinking of rain—a lie, going brief.

Now the yellow, now gray, of our many-many shapes:
    "In reputation there can be no effect." Yet some
    wire-draw their loving.

        In a sliver of light runs the past.

  I sit naked on the bed, outstanding like that.

WE SHOULD MEDDLE SOBERLY WITH JUDGING DIVINE ORDINANCES

Up and down the toil it swept me
Like if you hear starlight, how open
And what false bang of gods

Death makes an answer as love
Fills the dot
A lady in snow, a blank bird, a mouth

Yet time was just writing, maybe pursuit
It hung spotty from freeze
As proof I persist

"Strangeness itself lends credit"
No ordinary reason in the ice fields
This blizzard of symbol

"Blowing hot and cold with the same mouth"
The weapon of memory shattered in sun
Lift your eyes to its prick

ONE MAN'S PROFIT IS ANOTHER MAN'S HARM

Fortune was lack, of you
        lack, I won from you
the stubborn squad of gold. Singing a profit and in you
        the finite amount.

"Let each man sound himself within"
        or divvy the climate, in general policy
"the merchant does good business"
        and the banker
in ruin of houses
                                does good business.

VARIOUS OUTCOMES OF THE SAME PLAN

"He stood on a mound"
To be feared, fearing nothing
But weakness, remonstrance, "his nose happening to bleed"
With several passionate complainings

"He ought to have stuck to his text"

*

I didn't amble or jump
But bravely held to certain plans, certain arts
And entered the canvas

I believed in those faces floating in air . . .

A TRAIT OF CERTAIN AMBASSADORS

The point of the essay may be:

> to ramrod
> disabuse
> to instigate a kind of self-dawdle

OUR FEELINGS REACH OUT BEYOND US

Never at home, always beyond
Never present with, never in, never a cudgel
A cheap and easy reformation
Never daring, an error
The push our feelings do in the dark, not both
And behind them
Never occult, this relation to life
"Enfolding his companions"
Never a drum, their out-cries, ever frugal
Never a close-stool
"Nourishing modest humor"
Never the real bone, and buxom
Never dimensional, to feed
Speaking awe of natural violence
And of human

ONE IS PUNISHED FOR DEFENDING A PLACE OBSTINANTLY WITHOUT REASON

As a sentry
on the bridge
my position
against you
the world
lissome and angry
between us
very widely
around us
perhaps I was
ridiculous
or final
and strife
the gray puffs
between us
my sentry
a wolf
in the distance
a position
amongst them
I came to my power
like snow
a totally
intransigent time

in the manner
of trouble
I looked
to the bridge
"valor has its limits"
and our argument
"like other virtues"
a good taste
at times

HOW WE CRY AND LAUGH FOR THE SAME THING

I left it was various. As leaving spreads its prim canker. And keen through the air space. One sends the bcc. Thinking one feeds the light wholly. Though sun is a sin we have walked through to this. Our own skin. Is it scratching like walking. Or in jolly assembly. "I instantly turn over the leaf." With watery eye, soul picks at its movement. Blotchy, and fixed.

IT IS FOLLY TO MEASURE THE TRUE AND FALSE BY OUR OWN CAPACITY

Knowing the doubt I knew the mouse
Once at rest in my home I knew
The spirit who occupied
And me too I conceived
The trapless summer I saw
By its trap

So like an infant wall of belief
Climbing with ivy at night
I sat ringleted, this certain braid
In the spirit
And wreathed it
The stuff I knew lay beyond

Its rebuke was familiar
"To know the limits of possibility"
Spread of world
Spread of novelty
"My own swing and fancy"
Took nosegays for a cure

"NOW I AM ALL FACE"

The garden turned cold with our garb

Its long lovely lines

Simple words fashion a scarf

The sequence of huts

"In which they bury their fruit trees in winter"

Someone's in fun fur, just like a proverb

A tumbler of black wine

Tipped out and retaining its shape

That was my freak code, "the frosts

So bitter at the mouth"

OF SOLITUDE

I made some usual comparisons

My head to a bough, the stairs
to my dress

"Let us reply to ambition"

To keep the years I kept safely, in my way
in a crowd, to signal my quarrel
the glow or vibration

"There is nothing so un and so sociable as man"

In this I ran often, away
like a stain, insistence
I grew there

So the sun set there too

"Sequestered from the instincts inside us," I moved
counting beans in my back shop
—Forty-five, forty-six—

"Let us reply—"

small poof in the head

★

Palmed the false coin so you see it
every word performing an item
and boasting the status, my friends
our trials never enough
I took all of the trouble

⋆

But tucked away
shall I continue
or hide all of my stinging

Shall I dig there
make an adequate theater
"failing in solitude as well as company"

I felt myself open: "the frugal man, miser
the voluptuous man, and ambitious"
all rode into moblight

WONDER, THE CHASE, AMBIGUITY

WHITE MONEY AND RAGS

A long day of serious fucking
men and war

In sunshine, the raindrop
little mumble of mind

This is our fear and our manner of coming
our enemy's proem

"I put my trust easily in another man's word"
over hilltops with gallant array

A hazard plan, this hoop
and runaway spiel

TO FLEE FROM SENSUAL PLEASURES AT THE PRICE OF LIFE

Better to pray, retire
        "To bump up against the very laws of nature"
Lead away from the pack
        With feeling around me, all up on it
Or the cool spur of air
        Thrust from my life, it's a jeweled fist!

Knowing well those deft adornments
        Their alkaline twinkle
"At which he exhibited a singular joy"
        "But as for pushing the contempt of death"
Various thrills turn my face
    Solving the zero problem:

"To preserve life to our torment and discomfort"
        Thunder do you call
St. Hilary who killed his daughter, then his wife
        By prayer?

“THAT PROWESS DEPICTS US”

This was the vagabond freedom of pain

The animal doesn’t fear, and I had haunches

“A powerful performer, bold and immoderate”

I gave everything a lot of space, well occupied with considering

Completely certain in all my relations

Very full of mood

That little spirit

THAT INTENTION IS JUDGE OF OUR ACTIONS

A living hole

Monstrously popular

Incalculable, cold—

The far end of our kind

My thing so urgent and little

"Bound beyond our powers and means"

Think of the death we are making

“THAT WE USE OUR PRAYERS AS A JARGON”

Or as pebbles
          made of sea-light, fossils, error
Inscrutable, like a cottage
and getting lost inside

As one gorgeous shrub, pulled up
its texture somehow careful, then wet—time
          is over or I’m not
                    in it anymore

As I bear it, in the mouth

★

As the delicate temerity with which each leaf thunders
its data, “both crime and judge”

As God is lucid
and perched
in one’s central notions

How can the force
be lucid and I want it

As "this vain and verbal knowledge"
in my hour

*

As in trespass, and diversion indulging
          those multiple secrets
"what prodigy of a conscience can be at rest"

As the backyard and burn pit
                              As garden, refuse, myself
setting tables with china, and silver
                                        but no food on it

ALWAYS GIVE THE SOUL AN OBJECT

Always give the soul an object: cup, computer, piebald horse, or
a garden

Some flash surface to glide its thought upon

The drifting face of a lover, for example

This significantly wild, as the soul in love with "monkeys and
little dogs," raging against "salt meats"

"Chewing and swallowing cards"

A cannon ball, a locket—for example, one's lover who drinks

And common practice, to tear my hair then weep

A CONSIDERATION UPON CICERO

It's not history here, say the sages, but in "numberless proofs" and "ambitious nature" Cicero left behind his memos, and Pliny.

Who falters in doing and saying I'll do.

★

Stretch on the carpet of my floor, a lovely noodle.

"One has misspent one's leisure and study."

★

From philosophy I gleamed this letter of rec. But my language accosts another young inamorato.

★

"What are you, to play so brave? Are you a man-at-arms?
    Are you an archer?
    Are you a pikesman?"

★

Sometimes the moon is out my window, sometimes not; sometimes one silver hazard full in the street, walking my mouth.

⋆

"Fie on the eloquence that leaves us craving itself, not things!" On this subject I drove into town, a long-ass email at work in my head.

CEREMONY OF INTERVIEWS BETWEEN KINGS

A dear friend lays out this plate now that cup
What is appropriate between us?

Like who lessens and goes greater
With the saggy night around

Who fattens and who thins?
"Someone takes offense, I can't help it"

The visit is faithful so I become its pope
No, its Emperor at Marseilles

FEELINGS OF OF

OF MODERATION

The flat join corrupting
Bars of nickel, of kid, and petty living
"We by our handling corrupt things"
I was good up till then

"Learning shamelessness from another hand"
I extended my leg
Do you ignore it?

OF CANNIBALS

"Altering history a little," sameness moving along with my blood. What was natural, stuck to the skin, "calling wild as we call wild the fruits." And loved for things I could not do, attitude unpeeling like wood:

"No sort of traffic, no knowledge of letters, no science of numbers"
          "No occupations but leisure ones"

                    Someone wanders in bright pop of sun
My own example, grown harder

"I am sorry judging their faults rightly, so blind to our own"—
don't call it my head, floating sweetly like custom. Putting
thought into everyone

                    Open the door of the mountain
                    Its silver stick outraging there

OF A LACK IN OUR ADMINISTRATIONS

In all this system I watched a cloud fall
Carted wet down the design
Need is a big pool
Lo go its creaturely waves

Commerce came open and bright like a starfuck
"I hear, with great shame for our century"
Last zing on the stairs

"So-and-so wants company to Paris; so-and-so is looking for a
    servant with such-and-such qualifications"

Execution too diddled back then

"So and-so wants a master"

OF NOT COMMUNICATING ONE'S GLORY

One has some glory—brutal and rough, a kind of encounter
Fame is not pursuant

The splendid enterprise, peerage, and trench—
Let us consider that flourish

I had a friend who gloried, this seemed invisible to some
He broke apart his face, he promoted

"That was abandoning reputation to cover up shame"
As evening borrows its tickle from sun

And from retrospect, with alarm
"I don't know anyone has got clean rid of it"

OF THE INEQUALITY THAT IS BETWEEN US

Nothing looks out, you cannot see in—like flowers
"You don't buy a cat in a bag"

★

"All the advantages of princes are quasi-imaginary advantages"
Can there be too much love between us?

Pull off the side of this house
Measure me without my stilts

★

"There is more distance from a given man to a given man than
from man to an animal"

When I was branded a man I took my princely measure

Finery and pain at my outpost

OF WAR HORSES

In passable aloneness, the poison

"By volleys of kicks"

I hold this to the same reckoning, myself

"And seemed to have heard that the Romans had horses," and
    the Spaniards, the sylphs

Mounted at top speeds, "side by side without bridle or saddle"

In fullest career

The Numidian men-at-arms, the yokels and faghags

One Turk in my power

"Some day we shall abandon the use of it"

The Massilians, Assyrians, and Greeks

Gascons, Flemings, Picards, the douchebag heels

And Greeks

"I drew blood from their horse and used it for food and drink,"
    salting it

The Tartars, the knuckleheads, the Muscovites and hipsters, all
    called my neighing a language "of conciliation and truce"

The exes unbridled, and breaking

One drop of mare's milk fell on the mane, I licked it off with
    my tongue, terrible myth—

To be of the horses

On galloping rivers, it wasn't ever

Like I said

And indifferent, to submit

The timber

Going

Dark lid

OF DEMOCRITUS AND HERACLITUS

The evening was a durable motif—pearly then absorbing
There was the grey squirrel, zooming
A thing I treat according to

In the tests I make of judgment this cannot
Cross over—a judgment
Vain and nonexistent
Noble, well-worn   (it wasn't difficult to talk about
                                  anything here)

"I take the first subject that chance offers"
A face, member, a feeling
Of assortment, and hatreds—
Each pinching

Once I made a dog lick my hand, such was my lowliness
A function of the soul

OF THE VANITY OF WORDS

I was waving my reed

And among the very rabble

Loving the listening field, really feeling it

Puking up some oration, to be hearty

Guzzled, "but not speaking of actions, speaking"

What an instrument in my chest

Blurp, blurp

A light flatter

OF A SAYING OF CEASAR'S

One tries life and the glowing
Is a clever future, very plenty
"All built up of feeble"

With easy time gone gaping
The storm's a kind of high handsome thing—
"Forced to take part"

Then a crack—no a thrash—and deep
On the estate
Dishevelment stretched

Then whispered:
Ø animals in my household today
Ø children

OF AGE

The day comes crawling
I marry the theory
It's just river
Outside my laughable house
Become flowered

What is the duration
Its object
I go in search of—
The fruit is tiny and sharp
"The age one few people reach"

OF THE EDUCATION OF CHILDREN

I was planted, a crop
not a boy but with headlong technique, everything in me telling
to be coursed through with water and emptiness

⋆

The blank was worth tending
a matter of tight, small discretions
separating from youth like a bee

It's just silence
I've been talking about

Into hills I tried things I was made of
What was not in my memory, not math
yet patched all together
I required this armor
"wrestling with old champions body against body"

★

Scribbling down the solution
"by little light attacks"

A life is at odds and we solve it
a shadow itself

"Understanding makes profit of everything—arranges, acts, and
reigns,"
gives knowledge out in a swan

Virtue wasn't a mountain, not a field
or was it me brooding

*

"Too ill to instruct others,"
this awareness of slow moving and ditch
of the past of the subject

A few lumps on the ground like a book

"Mixing with men is wonderfully useful"
but hard practice

"For our boy, a closet, a garden, the table and bed, solitude, company, morning and evening, all hours will be the same, all places will be his study"

*

He's in philosophy, and mingled
let him forgive it
I have been happy in rooms

Gambling with pocket, with babble
"he will not say his lesson as do it"
and the unit is character,
"repeated in actions"

*

Rising to beg and confounding
I hear it now, in our ears

BUT THE SOUL IS LIGHT

THAT TO PHILOSOPHIZE IS TO LEARN TO DIE

Performing the rites
There will be this, in the aster
The milkweed the water
The wrong names
And we sort them
"'Tis the necessary object"
Our aim and traipsing
On the earthen bed
It's a small task
The starting-hole
Suspected country
"Rid of its strangeness"
The milk names
And beds
Which cannot moan, being lost
"I want at least as much more"
More exemplary, booted
And spurred
"This beautiful contexture
Of things"
And watery comforts
Happening once, can't it be
Terrible, a tilting
If less than this nothing
Or meadow between us—

"To live is at life's expense"
Like thought
Getting sillier
And flowers with dirt
So I think it

Paint a skull on my head
Bring me out
To the feast

OF VAIN SUBTLETIES

There's a school where I live
It's unused or misused and maybe by me, overrun
The vain part that goes there
To smoke and to see what is happy or sad, perhaps peace
In the playground considering how a metal slide might
Or a swing set, and Bermuda grass
The last time, a year ago, or a few months ago
I was happy and vague, the terrible
Place that will change, approximate to the wish
And quiet before
Where a person might sit on a bench and look out, remember
It's not like youth, though I want to be things
Creeping alive, and the perimeter
Alive, and the foxtail to stomp through, one must be happy
In content, to have lived
In a city
Its archive, not one or the other
"A marvelous testimony of weakness, our judgment"
It's a middle condition

The thought of what means
"An abecedarian ignorance, before knowledge"
And behind it, the loose field
Or equally troubling, where one walks
Not in love or a lover's old war

But through variety
A big blue and faint red, like "the nickname of 'The Trembler'"
Might also recommend us
"To endure human accidents"
There is a little impression I can understand
As monkey bars or utmost
Fear, and coming after experience
"In the middle range"
With an extensive depression, like looking
Even to walk back, turning in
Is going towards it, the doctrinaire passions
Stupid or royal to keep on

Regarding achievement, I've always
Used them
"Between two, without honor and value"
And noticed how formal my composition is
The snappy velvet of weed, my backpack, and
Mind, though
Right here the flattened down daisy
Takes over, or woodchip, a serious explanation
Whether it's being pretty
OK in the lens
As the spaces above and below pleasure, in retrospect
Filled an impossible certainty, so the dead
End, "our inventiveness warmed up"
Stops at the fence, to begin
Where one travels the passage

THAT OUR HAPPINESS MUST NOT BE JUDGED UNTIL AFTER OUR DEATH

One might like fine days of absolute nothing, just blue floating down in occasional handfuls, and leaving one's house for the moment, in the blue of going we watch you

"It is the master day, the day that is judge of all others": in this absolute there is nothing, a fine day, or knowing you turn your back to the street, precisely the last of the street you are going

That which is clean and good and present you have given away—"There is no more pretending" what's judicious though random, composing itself to perfection—

You are pink through the going

NOTE

M raids the first book of Michel de Montaigne's *Essays.* Quoted language in the poems is generally his, as are nearly all titles. "Of Fear" also contains language from *The New York Times, The New Yorker, Fox News Online, The National Review, The Economist,* and Hannah Arendt. I used three translations for this work: Donald Frame (1958), Charles Cotton (1685-86), and John Florio (1603). Speaking of her own citation-filled practice, Lorine Niedecker perhaps articulated the peculiarities of this method best: "All I could do is fill the subconscious and let it lie and fish up later. The hard part is to keep some quotes but not too many."

ACKNOWLEDGMENTS

My especial thanks to my parents, Laurel & Greg; to my siblings, Erin, Paul & Mara, Noah; to my grandmothers, Hazel & Bernice; to Stacy Jo Scott, my original collaborator; to Michele Christle, Emily Hunt, & Mollye Miller; to Peter Gizzi, Lisa Olstein, & Dara Wier; and to Ben Estes and Alan Felsenthal, who have been invaluable to these poems almost from their very start. Endlessly I thank Michel Montaigne. And more endlessly I thank Dan Bevacqua.

Versions of some of these poems first appeared in *Best American Experimental Writing,* the *Cambridge Literary Review, FENCE, iO, Prelude, Tammy, TH.CE, They Will Sew the Blue Sail, Typo,* and as a chapbook from the Song Cave. My sincere thanks to the editors of these journals.

OTHER TITLES FROM THE SONG CAVE:

1. *A Dark Dreambox of Another Kind*, by **Alfred Starr Hamilton**
2. *My Enemies*, by **Jane Gregory**
3. *Rude Woods*, by **Nate Klug**
4. *Georges Braque and Others*, by **Trevor Winkfield**
5. *The Living Method*, by **Sara Nicholson**
6. *Splash State*, by **Todd Colby**
7. *Essay Stanzas*, by **Thomas Meyer**
8. *Illustrated Games of Patience*, by **Ben Estes**
9. *Dark Green*, by **Emily Hunt**
10. *Honest James*, by **Christian Schlegel**